MathStart® AREA

Bigger, Better, BEST!

by Stuart J. Murphy • illustrated by Marsha Winborn

HarperCollins*Publishers*

LEVEL 2

To Maggie—who thinks her uncle is the best—Great Uncle Nick
—S.J.M.

The publisher and author would like to thank teachers Patricia Chase, Phyllis Goldman,
and Patrick Hopfensperger for their help in making the math in MathStart just right for kids.

HarperCollins®, 🏠 ®, and MathStart® are registered trademarks of HarperCollins Publishers. For more information about
the MathStart series, write to HarperCollins Children's Books, 10 East 53rd Street, New York, NY 10022,
or visit our website at www.mathstartbooks.com.

Bugs incorporated in the MathStart series design were painted by Jon Buller.

Bigger, Better, Best!
Text copyright © 2002 by Stuart J. Murphy
Illustrations copyright © 2002 by Marsha Winborn

Library of Congress Cataloging-in-Publication Data
Murphy, Stuart J.
  Bigger, better, best! / by Stuart J. Murphy ; illustrated by Marsha Winborn.
    p.   cm. — (MathStart)
  "Area."
  "Level 2."
  ISBN 0-06-028918-X — ISBN 0-06-028919-8 (lib. bdg.) — ISBN 0-06-446247-1 (pbk.)
  1. Area measurement — Juvenile literature.   [1. Area measurement.   2. Size.   3. Measurement.]   I. Winborn,
Marsha, ill.   II. Title.   III. Series.
  QA465.M85   2002   00-054034
  516—dc21

Typography by Elynn Cohen   10 11 12 13 SCP 10   ❖   First Edition

Jill shared a room with her older sister, Jenny. Their brother, Jeff, had a tiny room right across the hall.

Every morning when she woke up, Jill could hear Jeff and Jenny arguing.

"My backpack can hold more books than yours," Jeff said.

"But mine's purple, and yours is green. Purple's better," Jenny answered.

Jill stuck her head under the pillow.

Mine has an airplane.

5

Every night when she went to sleep, Jill could hear Jeff and Jenny arguing.

"My book's got more pictures than yours," Jenny said.

"But mine's got more pages," Jeff answered.

So what?

Mine's in color!

Oh, yeah?

Mine's in French.

Jill put her fingers in her ears. "My book's the best," she whispered to Fudge. "Look, it's about a cat just like you."

One day Mom and Dad announced that the family was going to move to a new house. The house was so big that Jill, Jenny, and Jeff could each have their own room.

"My room will be the best," said Jeff.

"No, mine will!" said Jenny.

"Will Fudge get his own room too?" asked Jill.
"Cats don't need their own rooms," said Mom.

Everyone wanted to see the new house, so they piled into the car. Jill brought Fudge.

When they got there, Jeff and Jenny ran right upstairs to see their rooms.

"Ha! I told you my room is better," Jenny said. "Look how big my window is."

— It's humongous!

"I've got a window too," said Jeff. "Bet mine is bigger."

"Stop arguing, you two!" said Mom.

"Here, take this pad of paper and cover your windows. If it takes more sheets to cover one of the windows, then you'll know that one has the larger area."

Jill helped Jeff tape sheets of paper
up one side of his window.
    "It's 3 sheets high," Jeff
announced.

Then he made as many rows as he could across the window.
"I can make 4 rows," he said. "That's 12 sheets of paper in all."

See? Mine's way bigger.

They ran to Jenny's room.

"My window is 2 sheets high. I can only make 2 rows," Jenny announced. "But it's really long."

She covered the entire window with sheets of paper. "I can fit 6 sheets across," she said. "That would make 12 sheets of window in all."

"Exactly the same," said Jill. "Can I have a piece of paper?"

"This is a pretty small room, Sis," said Jeff.

"I bet mine is bigger than yours."

"No, it's not," said Jenny.

"Yes, it is," said Jeff.

Uh-uh.

Yours is way smaller.

18

"Quiet down," said Dad. "That paper is too small. Here, you can use this old newspaper to see which room has the larger area."

Jenny taped sheet after sheet of newspaper along one of her walls.

"My room is 6 sheets wide," she announced.

Then Jill helped her tape sheets along the next wall.

"That's 5 sheets," said Jenny. "So if I covered the whole floor with newspaper, that would be 30 sheets in all."

"Well, I know my room's bigger," said Jeff. He grabbed the rest of the newspaper and ran to his room.

He taped sheets along one wall. "It's 6 sheets wide," he shouted.

Then Jeff put as many sheets as he could along the next wall. There were 4 sheets in all. "It would take 24 sheets to cover the whole floor," he said.

Mine's better!! I WIN!!!

"See, mine's bigger!" said Jenny.

23

"Wait," said Jill. "What about that little part in front of the closet?"

Jeff taped down more newspaper. There were 2 rows of 3 sheets each. "That's 24 sheets plus 6 sheets. That makes it 30 sheets in all!" Jeff said.

"Exactly the same *again*," said Jill. "Hey, look at this ad."

Sheesh.

Ha-ha, hee-hee!

25

"Well, my room's better than yours because it's closer to the bathroom," said Jenny.

"Ha," said Jeff. "Mine's better 'cause it's closer to the kitchen."

"You know what?" said Jill. "I think I have the best room in the house."

Jeff and Jenny looked at her in surprise.

"But your room is the smallest," Jenny pointed out.

"And you've just got one little window," Jeff added.

"I know," said Jill. "But my room is the farthest away from the two of you. And it's the closest to Fudge!"

In *Bigger, Better, Best!* the math concept is area. Area is a basic concept in geometry. It is measured in square units. As children learn about area, they are learning to visualize and calculate the number of square units that would be needed to completely cover the inside of a shape.

If you would like to have more fun with the math concepts presented in *Bigger, Better, Best!* here are a few suggestions:

- As you read the story, have the child count the number of pieces of paper needed to cover the windows and the floor in the illustrations. Tell the child that the children in the story are finding the area of the windows and the floor.

- Reread the story and point out that the children use paper of the same size when comparing the area of the two windows, and then use sheets of the same newspaper to find the area of the two bedrooms. To compare the area of shapes accurately, a consistent unit of measure must be used.

- Have the child draw a shape on a piece of graph paper. Together, count the squares inside the shape to find the area. Then help the child draw another shape that has the same area.

- Cut a piece of string as long as the child's arm. Use the piece of string to make a rectangle or a square. Have the child use square blocks to find the area of the shape. (All the blocks might not fit completely inside the string. In that case, the area can be expressed as a fraction—for example, $5\frac{1}{2}$ blocks.) Use the string to make other shapes and find their areas. Ask the child to find the shape with the largest area that can be made with the same piece of string.

Following are some activities that will help you extend the concepts presented in *Bigger, Better, Best!* into a child's everyday life:

Biggest Room in the House: Use newspaper to help the child find the area of his or her bedroom. Compare the area of the bedroom to the area of other rooms in the house. Remember to use the same size paper when comparing rooms.

In the Kitchen: Make brownies in two pans that are different sizes. Ask the child which pan is larger. Cut the brownies in each pan into squares that are the same size. Then have the child compare the area of each pan.

Refrigerator Art: Tape a piece of the child's art to the refrigerator. Have the child estimate how many projects of the same size it would take to cover the entire refrigerator door. Using the same size paper as the original piece of art, have the child figure out the solution.

The following books include some of the same concepts that are presented in *Bigger, Better, Best!*

- My Grandmother's Patchwork Quilt by Janet Bolton

- Spaghetti and Meatballs for All by Marilyn Burns

- Not Enough Room! by Joanne Rocklin